Your First
MOUSE

Nick C. Mays

CONTENTS

✧ DEDICATION ✦
To the memory of "the fab four":
Jackson, Violet, Minnie,
and Murgatroyd...
and all their many descendents!

Photos by Michael
Gilroy.

© 1996
By T.F.H.
Publications,
Inc., Neptune,
N.J. 07753 USA

———— • ————

T.F.H.
Publications,
The Spinney,
Parklands,
Denmead,
Portsmouth
PO7 6AR
England

Introduction

On the face of things, a mouse seems to be a very small and insignificant mammal. It is not a voracious hunter but is itself hunted by countless predators, from tawny owls to giant toads, from cats to corn snakes. It is not exactly a plant eater either. No, the mouse is more of a scavenger, picking up what it can, where it can. Yet, for all this, the house mouse, *Mus Musculus*, is one of the most successful animal species on the face of the earth. Why? The answer is simple: from its points of origin in Asia, the mouse—remaining largely unseen—quickly spread out and colonized the world alongside man. Wherever man settled, there the mouse settled. Every village, town, and city in the world has colonies of mice within its dwellings, or underground, or in grain stores, warehouses, and factories. Yes, the mouse is a very successful animal, although often a much maligned one also. Because of their scavenging and gnawing activities, mice have been classified as vermin, as indeed have most members of the order Rodentia, to which the mouse belongs.

But there are other sides to the mouse. There is a particular fascination about it. Countless stories have been written about mice, many of them classics: *Mrs. Frisby and the Rats of Nimh,* by Robert O'Brien; *The Tale of Mrs. Tittlemouse, The Tale of Two Bad Mice,* and *The Tale of Johnny Town Mouse* by Beatrix Potter; and, predating all of them by some 2,000 years, Horace's famous story of the Town Mouse and his cousin the Country Mouse. In entertainment, mice make great cartoon characters. Everyone must have seen the wily Jerry running rings around his hapless foil Tom the cat in the Tom and Jerry cartoons. Then there is the most famous celluloid mouse of them all: Mickey Mouse, created by Walt Disney in 1928 and still going strong today. But quite apart from all of this, although perhaps keeping the entertainment angle in mind, mice make great pets for young and old alike.

Mice have been domesticated for many hundreds of years, the earliest domesticated specimens being recorded in the royal palaces of ancient China and Japan. Thanks to the surge of interest in mice and exhibition livestock in the late 19th century, many new colors and varieties were developed, which have enabled domesticated mice, like their wild ancestors, to spread all around the world.

CLASSIFICATION

The mouse, like all other animals and plants, is scientifically classified under the universally accepted classification system. There are many different species of mice which, being rodents, are all related. However, the species with which we are concerned is *Mus musculus,* the house mouse. This is how we arrive at this conclusion:

Phylum: Chordata—with a backbone

Class: Mammalia—mammals, animals that suckle their young

Sub-class: Eutheria—animals with a placenta

Order: Rodentia—gnawing animals

Sub-order: Simplicidentata—possessing one pair of "chisel-like" upper teeth

Infra-order: Myomorpha—of mouse-like shape

Family: Muridae—mice and rats

Genus: *Mus*—mice

Species: *musculus*—the house mouse

In short: *Mus musculus*

MICE AS PETS

The first western domesticated mice were used in laboratories in scientific research. Using the humble mouse, man has researched such diverse scientific fields as diseases, genetics, behavior, stress...the list is seemingly endless. Even today, mice and rats are the animals most widely used in scientific research, more so than any other animal. However, as previously mentioned, mice have been kept as pets for many thousands of years in the Orient, so the idea quickly caught on in the West.

The idea of a pet mouse has become a sort of cliché; it brings to mind the image of a scruffy schoolboy taking his pet white mouse to school in his pocket and frightening all the "yucky" schoolgirls with it, as a hilarious alternative to dipping their pigtails in the inkwells. If he is admonished by his teacher—a middle-aged, waspish female—he shows her the mouse; whereupon she promptly leaps up onto her chair, holding her skirts, screaming. But there is more to mice as pets than merely to frighten swooning females. In fact, females of all ages can and do keep mice as pets as easily as their male counterparts. Mice may not be cuddly or loving, but they are interesting. They are easy to house, cheap to feed, extremely easy to breed, available in a wide range of attractive colors and markings, are easily tamed, and are far less demanding than other larger pets.

The only real drawback that mice have is that they are not very long-lived animals. The average lifespan of a mouse is between 1 year and 18 months. During this time, however, they can give a lot of pleasure as pets.

Selection

Before embarking on purchasing your first mouse—or indeed any other pet animal—you must first ask yourself a few basic questions:

Why do you want a mouse? Do you want it purely as a pet or as a show animal?

Do you want to keep one mouse, or more?

If you are keeping several mice, what sex will they be?

If you will be keeping mice of both sexes, you will presumably be breeding them. Can you be sure of finding homes for the offspring?

If the mouse is for a child, can you be sure (a) that the child wants a mouse, (b) whether he will continue to care for it once the novelty has worn off, and (c) that if the child in question is not yours, his parents will give their permission for him to keep a mouse?

Having considered all of these points and if you have answered positively in each case, now you are ready to actually go out and select your pet. For the sake of simplicity in this chapter, let us assume that you are aiming to keep one mouse. All the information given herein applies to individual mice and would be the same no matter how many you were getting.

OBTAINING A MOUSE

First of all, where to obtain your mouse? Do not even be tempted by the ridiculous statements in some books in which it is stated that wild-caught mice will tame nicely and make good pets. *They do not!* Quite apart from the tameness factor, wild mice carry all kinds of unpleasant parasites and often a fair selection of diseases (admittedly through no real fault of their own); so it is pointless to even think of keeping them. Domesticated mice are clean and tame—definitely not to be confused with their wild relatives.

Naturally most people think of the pet shop as a source of mice, and they're right: most pet shops stock mice. Before you make your purchase, there are some important factors that must be considered. For instance, are the mice kept in mixed sex colonies? If so, the chances are that you may end up with a pregnant female. If you do not want to breed mice, this could be a big problem. Also, look carefully at the seller's facility. Is it clean, bright, and well organized? Are all the animals housed in clean accommodations in bright, cheerful surroundings? Can the staff provide the information that you need? Again, ask some

The mouse, like all other animals and plants, is scientifically classified under the universally accepted classification system. There are many different species of mouse, which, being rodents, are all related. This book deals with *Mus musculus*, the house mouse, which is the most commonly found species of mouse. Photo by Michael Gilroy.

questions. Can they sex the mice? How old are the mice? What is their preferred diet, etc.? Does the staff seem nervous about handling the mice, or do the mice themselves seem nervous? If these questions can be answered in a positive manner, you can then proceed.

If your pet shop does not have the particular color variety that you want, perhaps the dealer can special order it for you. If not, maybe you can contact a local mouse breeder. Of course, this is not as easy as it sounds, because very few mouse breeders are listed in the phone book. A possible point of contact is through a mouse club. Details of such clubs can be obtained from registers of clubs and societies, which are available in your local library. Alternatively, you can write to the author care of T.F.H. Publications, PO Box l5, Waterlooville, PO7 6BQ, England. Please remember to enclose a stamped self-addressed envelope or International Reply Coupon as appropriate.

Once you have made contact with a breeder, you can pay him a visit. Remember to ask him the relevant questions about your mouse: its age, sex, hereditary background, preferred housing, best food, etc. If you do visit a breeder, also remember to bring a strong box or another type of suitable container in which to collect your mouse: breeders do not always keep a supply of such containers nor should you expect them to.

WHAT TO LOOK FOR

The average mouse should measure some 4 in. (10 cm) in length, excluding the tail, which should be as long as the body. Of course, there are many different varieties from which to choose, but the general "type" of a mouse is the same. The coat should be even and clean, with no bald patches. Whether the coat is long or short, it should be smooth and glossy. Of course, satinized mice have extra glossy coats, but the general rule applies. Curly-coated mice often have natural "baldness" when young, so make allowances for this—here you will need to be guided by what the seller tells you. Check that there are neither parasites in the fur, nor flaky skin. The mouse's ears should be large and erect—in fact, almost tulip-shaped, as specified in the mouse judging standards. The eyes should be bold, bright and clear, and free from any dullness or discharge. The nose should be clean and twitching, the whiskers long and full. The tail should be clean and free of scabs or bites. Also, run your index finger and thumb along the mouse's tail, checking for kinks. If you intend to use the mouse for breeding, a badly kinked tail will lead to a genetical fault in the offspring: they too will have kinked tails. Also, a show mouse will be disqualified because of this fault. Look at each foot in turn, checking carefully that all of

A mother mouse keeps watch over her newly born litter. If you are planning to keep male and female mice, you will presumably be planning to breed them. This means that you will have the responsibility of finding homes for the youngsters that you do not keep. Photo by Michael Gilroy.

the toes are intact. The mouse
should be pleasantly sleek—
neither thin or wasted, nor
overweight. An obese mouse
will not have good health
prospects. If a female mouse
(doe) is extra large over the
flanks, then chances are that
she is pregnant; so, unless you
want lots of baby mice, avoid
buying her. Finally, observe how
the mouse behaves. It should be
alert and reasonably active. It
should not be skittish or
nervous. If a mouse bites when
approached, have nothing to do
with it as a pet.

One very important factor to
bear in mind is smell. Despite
what some books say, mice do
smell. Males (bucks) have a
particularly strong odor, and this
must be borne in mind when
selecting either a single mouse
or a single-sex pair. Does have
a slight smell, but it is not nearly
as noticeable as in bucks. If you
do want a single-sex pair of
mice, then two does will do
nicely. Not only would two bucks
smell more strongly, but also the
chances are that they would
fight for supremacy as well.

As previously mentioned,
mice are not really cuddly or
loving pets, so do not expect to
see your mouse run up to its
handler, licking him and trying to
snuggle up to him. However, the
sign of a good mouse is one that
will sit calmly but remain alert, or
climb around on its handler
without any sign of fright or
panic. This, then, is the mouse
for you!

Pet shops stock a variety of cages from which you can choose. The model shown here is lightweight and easily transportable. Its only drawback is that it is of the "spoke" variety, which can cause tail injuries. A wheel with a solid back is much safer. Photo by Dr. Herbert R. Axelrod.

Housing

Being relatively small animals, mice do not need tremendously large or complicated housing. Most pet shops stock a wide variety of cages, many specifically designed for mice, that will be perfectly suitable.

WHAT TYPE OF CAGE?

One of the most popular mouse cages is the kind with a sturdy plastic or metal base and a wire canopy over the top. This type of cage is not only attractive but also easy to clean and enables you to see your mouse. The minimum cage size for one mouse or a pair of mice is 12 in. x 8 in. x 8 in. (30 cm x 20 cm x 20 cm). As mice are adept at squeezing through small spaces, the bar gauge—the space between the bars—should be no more than $\frac{3}{8}$ in. (8 mm). Often, this type of cage is sold as a hamster cage, whereby the bar gauge is somewhat wider, so make sure that you get the right gauge.

Another suitable type of cage is one that is made of either metal or thick wood, with solid sides and a sliding glass front. Sometimes the glass front extends up to two-thirds of the cage's height, with the remainder of the area being metal bars. Again, the minimum dimensions apply. Often, this type of cage has a nest box fitted on the inside, with a ladder running up to it. This is ideal, as mice like to climb and also enjoy a secure nest area. However, experience shows that a nest box without a lid or roof is preferable, as nest boxes often overheat when packed with bedding and mice!

Aquarium tanks, constructed of either plastic or glass, make excellent cages for mice. The advantage of an aquarium tank is that it affords all-around vision and also serves to keep the occupants warm and snug, safe from drafts. Conversely, of course, it is necessary to ensure that the tank is not placed in direct sunlight or a hot area, as the greenhouse effect takes on a whole new meaning and the occupants will suffer! Obviously, an aquarium tank will need a lid. Often such tanks come complete with a lid; but it is best to discard it, as what may be suitable for fish is not suitable for mice. A proper lid does not allow for the necessary ventilation. Instead, you will need to construct a lid out of small-gauge wire—the more solid, the better. Chicken wire breaks up too easily, and often a persistent mouse can actually gnaw through it or make the holes in the chicken wire bigger and thus escape. Mice are nothing if not persistent...so beware of the activities of the "escape committee."

BASIC CAGE REQUIREMENTS

To start with, you need substrate—a covering for the floor. Sawdust is by far the best substrate for mice. Wood shavings are also acceptable, but experience shows that mice prefer a finer, softer floor covering, sawdust being ideal. It is always best to purchase sawdust direct from a pet shop, where it will be—or should be—packaged in pre-medicated bags. Of course, you can buy sawdust direct from a lumberyard but beware of large splinters and be mindful of running the risk of contamination or of foreign bodies in the sawdust.

Mice like to make nests, so bedding is definitely required. Ignore what you may have read about shredded newspaper being acceptable—it is not. Printed paper can be toxic to small animals. Once again, your pet shop should be able to meet your requirements for bedding. Avoid fiber-based bedding, especially those with a nylon base. The fibers are hard and sharp and can cause horrific injuries to small animals, such as severing toes or feet. Soft shredded paper makes ideal bedding and is not expensive. This kind of paper, of course, is not printed and is often pre-medicated. The very best bedding is hay. Not only is it warm, but also the mice can eat it, and it provides good roughage in their diet.

A food bowl is another necessary item. It will preferably be a solid earthenware or metal kind that cannot easily be tipped over. Plastic bowls are tippable and, not surprisingly, also get chewed up very quickly. Water is best provided by using a gravity water bottle as opposed to a bowl, which can get filled with sawdust and thus soak up all the water, not to mention making a mess. Bottles are provided with special hangers for most cages. If your mouse is housed in an aquarium tank, it is a fairly simple matter to make a "cradle hanger" out of wire, in which the bottle can be suspended from the wire-mesh lid and hooked over the side of the tank.

FURNISHINGS

Many commercially made cages come complete with certain basic furnishings such as nest boxes. If your cage does not have any such furnishings, then it is up to you to provide them. Often nest boxes can be bought separately—small bird nest boxes can be used. Plastic hamster houses may also be used but may be gnawed. Again, be mindful of the fact that the box is best without a lid. Alternatively, you can just leave it to the mice by providing them with plenty of bedding material. They will choose where to make a nest, usually in the corner of the cage.

Mice do not really go in for toys as such—they are not ultra-intelligent animals requiring "play stimulation." However, cardboard tubes from toilet tissue and paper towel rolls are often used as makeshift "burrows" and are also relished for gnawing activities. Regarding the matter of gnawing, mice, being rodents, do need to exercise their chisel-like incisor teeth. Recent studies, in laboratories using mice as their experimental animals, have shown the **Nylabone**® and **Chicken Nylabone**®, made for dogs, are superb for mice to gnaw away their teeth and exercise problems. Every pet shop carries Nylabone®. If the mice do express a desire to gnaw—but not all mice do— then this will prevent them from gnawing on parts of their cage.

Mice are quite acrobatic, and you will get used to the sight of one walking upside down underneath the cage lid or climbing the bars. A couple

Above and below:
These Nylabone® products are ideal as pacifiers and tooth gnaws for all kinds of rodents, especially mice.

All pet shops carry complete assortments of dog chews that are also perfect for mice.

of ladders will always be appreciated. They can be bought from a pet shop, where they are sold for use by birds such as budgies and cockatiels. With the gnawing factor in mind, it is best to avoid plastic ladders and instead choose metal ones. Also, a strict ladder structure is not totally necessary. A branch or thick twig does just as well. Make sure that you wash branches and twigs before giving them to the mice. In time, they will probably get gnawed away, but the beauty of this is that they can be replaced easily.

Swings are also welcome and can be hung from the top of the cage or lid. Again, bird accessories—in this case, swings (metal)—are ideal.

EXERCISE WHEELS

Many cages come complete with exercise wheels, which are useful, as many mice enjoy taking a spin on them. Some wheels are pathetically small, even for mice. The best rule of thumb is "the bigger, the better," so a wheel that allows a mouse to trundle around in it without being cramped or hunched is perfect. It is best to use a solid wheel as opposed to the "spoke" variety, as nasty accidents with trapped tails can occur.

CAGE LOCATION

Situate the cage in a stable area, where the occupants are protected from drafts, direct sunlight, or excessive heat. The optimum "room temperature" range for mice is between 15 and 19° C (59 and 66°F). Also, ensure that the cage cannot be knocked down or the occupants molested by young children or other household pets, such as cats and dogs. On no account should a mouse cage be kept outside, unless it is in a shed or outbuilding. Not only is this dangerous with predators about, but also it is asking for trouble with temperature fluctuation. Mice may be hardy, by and large, but they cannot withstand extremes of temperature or dampness.

Feeding

When considering the correct diet for your mouse, it is necessary to forget all the old wives' tales and cartoon baloney about mice living on cheese. Most mice—even wild ones—do not like cheese anyway, as it is often far too strong in flavor and smell for their palates. Like any other pet animal, your mouse requires a well-balanced diet that is suitable for its needs. What it may eat might not seem attractive or interesting to you, but it is what is good for the mouse that is important.

BASIC DIET

The bulk of the mouse's diet consists of dry food. The best combination of this is clipped or rolled oats, mixed corn, flaked maize, and dried crushed peas. Usually, you can obtain a good basic dry food mixture from your pet shop. It may be either in the form of a proprietary brand or something that the shop mixes itself. With the prepared brands, it is necessary to check the contents carefully. A dry mix can contain a large proportion of rabbit pellets, sunflower seeds, and peanuts. Often mice totally reject the rabbit pellets on the grounds of taste. Sunflower seeds and peanuts will, however, be readily eaten; but as both are very rich in protein,

this can cause problems. Too much protein can "overdose" in a mouse and lead to sores and spots on the skin and loss of condition. A few of these items in the mix are all well and good; but if they are the dominant

A dry food mix consisting of oats, sunflower seeds, and bits of dog biscuit. When it comes to your mouse's diet, the best thing to do is to stick to the basic mix and occasional fruit/vegtable supplements and try alternate foodstuffs from time to time. The main thing is to be sensible about what you are doing because the key to good health is good feeding. Photo by E. Jukes.

constituents, you are asking for trouble. To ensure that your mouse receives the correctly balanced dry food, it may be advisable to buy the different constituents and make up a mix yourself. Alternatively, the pet shop may make you up a mix on bulk order.

Sometimes, a proprietary mix contains dog biscuits. This is good, as dog biscuits are useful in giving the mice something extra to gnaw and are also quite nutritious. If the mix does not contain them, you can always buy a few to add or just leave them in the cage for the mice to gnaw when the mood strikes them. Always remember to remove them after a couple of days, however, in case they go moldy.

Stale bread is also a good, integral part of the diet. Do not worry about the fact that the bread is stale; this makes it harder, which the mice prefer. Be sensible about the degree of staleness however: no more than five days. Otherwise mold will probably develop.

GREENS

As a supplement to the basic diet, some greens, in the form of fruit or vegetables, may be given to your pets. Quite apart from the vitamins that such foodstuffs contain, they also contain a good degree of moisture. Avoid the different types of lettuce, as they have very little nutritional value and can be the main cause of diarrhea. Root crops such as carrot, turnip, and swede are good and filling. Cabbage and sprouts are acceptable, as are peas, spinach, watercress, and cauliflower leaves. More "natural" greenfoods can include chickweed, dandelion, and fresh young grass shoots. If you are picking any kind of vegetable from your own garden, make sure that you wash it thoroughly before feeding to your mice.

In fact, washing all greens is basic hygiene, especially as many commercially produced items are sprayed with pesticides. On the fruit front, the best fruit by far is apple, with tomato as second best. Citrus fruits should be avoided, as they contain a high level of citric acid, which can be harmful to small animals' stomachs.

Any greens should be given sparingly and then only as a supplement to the basic diet. Additionally, they should not be given too frequently: once or twice a week is perfectly acceptable.

DRINKING WATER

Although greens may contain a high level of moisture, always ensure that your mouse has clean fresh water every day. In warm weather, mice do drink a lot, as they can dehydrate very quickly with their fast metabolism. Occasionally, a bowl of bread and milk provides a welcome change, being a good source of vitamin B and calcium. Bread can also be soaked in water and placed in a bowl as an additional source of moisture when required—perhaps during hot weather or when you are away for a day or two, thus ensuring that the mice have adequate food and moisture at all times.

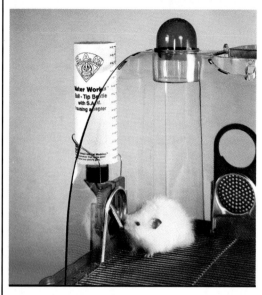

A gravity-fed water bottle, such as the one this hamster is using, is the ideal way to provide your mouse with water. Photo courtesy of Penn Plax.

Pregnant or nursing mice will also appreciate some bread and milk, which helps the mother build up her energy reserves. Also, young mice will develop quickly with access to this supplement.

VITAMINS AND MINERALS

Provided that your mouse receives a well-balanced diet, additional vitamins and minerals are not necessary. Cod-liver oil may be given sparingly, usually in bread and milk, to improve condition. This is especially useful in cold weather. Wheat germ extract can be added to the dry mix from time to time to improve condition by providing vitamin B. Such additives are especially valuable to pregnant or nursing mothers and young mice.

OTHER FOODS

By all means feel free to experiment with different foods and find out which suit your mouse or mice best. Some mouse fanciers have reared excellent mice on poultry mash, or even by making up their own "mashes" from bread, wheat germ, minerals, and vegetables. A mash is best fed in the winter months, especially if your mouse is housed in a shed or outbuilding. The best thing to do is to stick to the basic mix and occasional fruit/vegetable supplements and try alternate foodstuffs from time to time. The main thing is to be sensible about what you are doing because the key to good health is good feeding. An old fancier's saying sums it up: "Condition goes in through the mouth."

General Care

When you first bring your mouse home, put it in its cage with a supply of food and water and then leave it alone for a few hours. This will allow the mouse to explore its new home and get acquainted with the layout of things. Mice are territorial creatures, especially males (bucks); and they often mark their territory in the same way as other animals, by urinating or defecating in strategic areas. Generally, however, your mouse will reserve a particular area of the cage for its toilet. As mentioned earlier, bucks do have a rather pungent urine odor, but this is much less noticeable with females.

TAMING AND TRAINING

The first stage in fully taming your pet is getting it used to a regular routine and, more importantly, to you. Mice have an excellent sense of smell and can quickly identify their owners in this way. Also, your body language plays a great part in putting the mouse at ease. Inexperienced people often make sharp, nervous movements that unsettle the mouse. So, be slow and gentle

A Blue Fox. If housed adequately and given the correct diet, your mouse will require very little maintenance. Of course, it is necessary to keep an eye on its general health and well-being; but apart from that, your mouse can pretty well look after itself. Photo by E. Jukes.

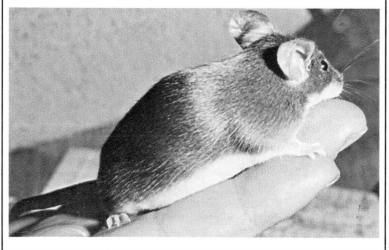

Screen covers are designed to fit any size tank. Some are equipped with devices that will insure the safety of the pet. Photo courtesy of Four Paws.

in your movements near the cage. Talk to the mouse, not just when you are feeding it, but whenever you are near it. Although the mouse will not understand a word that you are saying, it will associate your voice with you. In this way, the mouse can build up a picture of you via smell, movement, and sound. Its eyesight is not good so it won't recognize you visually, other than by your bodily movements.

After two or three days, your mouse should be sufficiently calm and sure of you for you to attempt the next stage of the procedure. The way to any animal's heart is through its stomach, so put a tasty tidbit of food between your finger and thumb and then offer it to the mouse through the bars of the cage, or from above. The mouse will probably sniff at you and the food; and then, if it feels safe enough, it will take the tidbit in its mouth and scurry off to eat it. Try this method three or four times until the mouse is fully at ease. It might even run up to the cage bars or stand on its hind legs when it sees you approach. Now put your hand in the cage, with the tidbit on your palm. Don't move, especially not suddenly—let the mouse come to you. With a bit of luck, it will hop onto your hand and take the tidbit. Hopefully, it will become sufficiently brave to eat the tidbit while sitting on your palm. Remember to quietly talk to it all the time to reassure it.

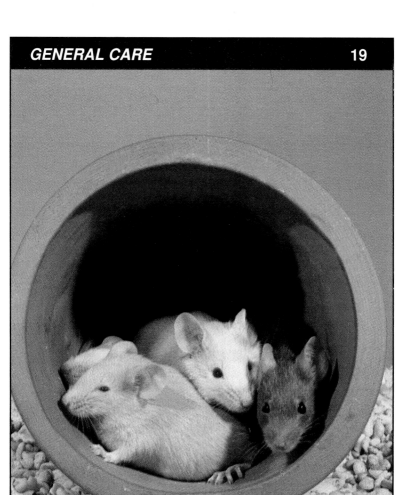

Properly cared for, a mouse can make a very interesting pet. It will compensate for its short life span (on the average between 1 year and 18 months) by packing a lot of activity into its life, and thus it will give you a great deal of enjoyment and amusement. Photo by Michael Gilroy.

Try this again two or three times to gain the mouse's confidence.

When you next attempt this and the mouse sits on your palm, gently close your fingers around the mouse's midriff and lift it up. If it panics, it may nip you—accept this—and then put it down again. Once more, try putting your fingers around it until you can lift it out of the cage. You can hold the tail close to its base to keep the mouse from jumping off your palm. By now, the mouse should be very confident, so let it run along your arm. It is a good idea at this stage to sit on a chair or a sofa and let the mouse run on you. Let it wander off onto the chair or sofa but be ready to grab it if it decides to make a break for freedom. Stroke the mouse gently and keep talking to it. In a short space of time, the mouse should be tame and confident in your company.

For speed and convenience, mice may also be picked up by their tails but only do this to transfer them to your palm or to the cage. *Always* remember to grasp the tail close to its base, or root. If you hold the mouse by the tip of its tail, this will hurt the mouse; and you may incur its wrath. Also, the tail may "skin," which is very painful for the mouse.

Some folks like to "train" their pets (although I'm not a lover of performing animals).

Of the rodents, *rats* are the most intelligent and thus the easiest to train, performing all kinds of entertaining tricks like running up ladders and hoisting flags, invariably for an edible reward. On a more scientific note, rats are often used in laboratory experiments studying behavior and learning. Mice, although capable of learning elementary routines, are not the most intelligent of rodents and so cannot learn to perform such complex tasks. However, if you really want to try teaching your mouse some tricks and you are prepared to put in several hours' effort, then why not?

Remember to keep the edible treat factor in the mouse's mind, and you may manage to teach it to climb up ropes or ladders to obtain a reward. It might also be fun for you to construct a mini-maze out of cardboard or plastic tubes and cardboard strips. You can create walls and corridors, down which the mouse has to run to find its reward. So long as you do not expect too much, like the mouse fetching your slippers for you, training your pet mouse can be an interesting experience.

CARING FOR YOUR MOUSE

If housed adequately and given the correct diet, your mouse will require very little maintenance. Of course, it is necessary to keep an eye on its general health and well-being; but apart from that, your mouse can pretty well look after itself.

You will need to clean out the cage once a week, giving it a complete change of sawdust and bedding. Pay particular attention to the corners of the cage, where dirty sawdust and feces can gather. A wallpaper scraping tool can come in handy here, reaching the parts that other tools cannot reach. About once every three months, give the cage a thorough washing with warm, soapy water and mild disinfectant. Then rinse it out, dry it and replace all the furnishings as before. It may be necessary to give the furnishings a cleaning in the same way, and this can form part of the quarterly clean up.

As long as you stick to the necessities of care, you can fully enjoy and appreciate your mouse as a pet.

BREEDING

Mice are counted among the most prolific of animals. They have a high fertility rate, a short gestation period, and reach maturity very quickly. Without trotting out that old chestnut about how many offspring may descend from an original pair of mice, suffice it to say that uncontrolled breeding can be a grave error. Quite apart from any other consideration, it is not fair to the mice. Before you start on the process of breeding your mice—and we shall assume for this chapter that you have at least a true pair of mice—you must consider a few questions similar to those asked when you decided to keep mice in the first place:

Do you have enough cages for this project? You will need one each for a buck and doe in a pair, possibly more if you have other does. You will also need at least one other to house the offspring when they are weaned.

Do you have the means of finding homes for the surplus offspring? You certainly will not want to keep them all.

If you do intend to sell excess mice, are you doing it hoping to make an income from it? If so, forget it—unless you own a mouse farm with hundreds of customers queuing up to buy your mice to the point of placing advance orders. Nobody ever made their fortune from mice! (Except, perhaps, Walt Disney...)

And especially for the younger reader: Make sure that you obtain your parents' permission before you embark on this course of action!

THE MATING PROCESS

Mice reach sexual maturity between 6 and 12 weeks of age, but it is best not to breed them too young. The usual breeding formula is to "run" a buck with two or more does. It is not simply a matter of leaving them all together to allow nature to take its course—breeding mice is a far more precise science than that. To begin with, breeding adults should be selected with a number of important factors in mind: size, stamina, and type (the actual shape and composition of the mouse by which all mice are initially judged), to say nothing of careful selection for the required variety. These points all come with experience, so do not expect to know it all from the word go. If you are interested in exhibiting fancy mice and want to breed some good specimens, *ask* some more experienced fanciers.

Initially, the buck should be housed on his own. You can then introduce one or more does to him as required. Ovulation in mice lasts between four and six days, with the heat lasting for up to 12 hours. At this time, the doe is at the peak of fertility, and the buck will quickly mate with her. Pregnancy is soon very noticeable, with the doe's body swelling greatly, especially over the flanks. At this point, the doe is said to be "in kindle" and may now be removed to her own cage to have her litter, or "to kindle." Unless you want wall-to-wall mice, do not leave the removal of the doe or buck until after the litter is born. Mice are subject to a condition known as "postpartum estrus." That is, the doe goes into heat immediately after the litter is born,

whereupon the buck will immediately mate her again.

It is a fallacy to say that buck mice will always eat a newborn litter. In fact, many make good fathers, even nestling down with the babies while the doe takes a breather. However, it is always best to follow the rules and separate the prospective parents before the litter is born. This prevents the undue strain on the doe of being pregnant while rearing the first litter. Her bodily resources will be divided between both litters, born and unborn, with the result that neither litter will enjoy optimum development.

GESTATION

Mice have a short gestation period, lasting between 18 and 21 days. During the last few days of pregnancy, it is necessary to provide the doe with extra bedding and also to increase her amount of food, perhaps adding some extra wheat germ, together with bread and milk. If you have two or three pregnant does, they may be allowed to litter together in the same cage, as long as the litters will be born within a couple of days of each other, so that all the babies are at roughly the same stage of development. Two or more does will often make a communal nest and suckle all the babies together. Obviously this method is to be avoided if you want to be sure which babies belong to a particular doe, in which case she should be housed on her own.

Mice mating. The doe "freezes" to allow the buck to mount her. If you decide to breed mice, then, from your original pair or trio, you can create your own mouse dynasty and chart the development of colors and markings throughout each generation. Photo by Michael Gilroy.

THE LITTER

The doe will give birth to her litter usually in the evening or early hours of the morning. Each baby is delivered in an individual birth sac, which the doe bites off and eats. She then cleans up the baby and adds it to the nest. The babies are born naked, blind, and deaf, able only to suckle from their mother. The average litter size is between 8 and 10, although litters of up to 18 are not unknown!

It is best not to disturb the nest for a day or two, even if the doe is a placid and trusting mouse. Instances of does eating their offspring are fairly rare; but, if a nursing mother panics, she may do just that—to protect her litter. Also, the doe may well dispose of any dead or sickly offspring herself, getting the litter to a manageable size.

The babies grow quickly; and after a few days, their ears open and they squeak more frequently, perhaps in a form of communicating with each other. The fur begins to grow at around four days, and markings on any marked or patterned varieties should also become apparent at this time. The babies' eyes open at 14 days, and they begin to scurry around. Often, the poor doe gets quite harassed and has to carry her babies back into the nest, rather like a female cat does with her kittens. The babies can start nibbling at solid food at around ten days of age and quickly learn to seek food out, although they will continue to suckle for about another ten days. At this point, remember to provide extra food for the babies. A bread-and-milk mixture is an ideal supplement to give them added calcium and vitamin B and thus promote their growth and development. The litter should be weaned between 21 and 28 days of age and removed to their own cage.

After this, you will find it necessary to sex them. Sexing mice is easy; the best method is to hold the mouse up by the tail and inspect the groin area. The distance between the urethra and anus is greater in bucks than in does. Does also have two rows of nipples, which are often quite visible, down their abdomen. Remember that mice reach sexual maturity very quickly, so the bucks and does must be split up into single-sex groups no later than six weeks of age. Mice are considered to be fully adult at eight weeks of age, which is in keeping with their relatively short lifespan.

The doe, now having raised her litter, can be returned to "public life" but must be rested for a couple of weeks to allow her to build up her bodily reserves and get back into condition before attempting to mate her again. Carefully used, a good doe can produce up to ten litters in her lifetime. Bucks can often remain virile until the day they die, but generally speaking, virility fades after 12 to 14 months.

As this duo demonstrates, mice are agile, acrobatic little animals. They use their tails for balance. Photo by Michael Gilroy.

Varieties

There are over forty different varieties of domesticated, or fancy, mice, which have been developed over the past 100 years. Some of the varieties are extremely rare nowadays, and some are still being developed.

The different varieties of mice are grouped together under different "type" classifications: Self (one color); Tan (with a Tan-colored belly); Marked (Patterned Varieties); A.O.V., Any Other Variety (varieties not covered by the other classifications); and Coat Varieties (mice with different fur types). Each individual variety then conforms to its own particular Standard of Excellence. In the UK, these Standards are laid down by the National Mouse Club, the governing body of the mouse fancy in that country. In the US, one of the largest organizations for mouse fanciers is the American Fancy Rat and Mouse Association. In a book this size, it would be impossible to list every individual variety and its full standard. What follows is a basic description of the varieties that you are more likely to find in a pet shop.

SELFS

Basically, Selfs are mice with one overall body color and no other markings. The eye color varies in varieties, depending on certain genetical traits relating to that color. For instance, you may well find white mice with either pink or black eyes. The pink-eyed specimens are true albinos, that is, animals with no coloration whatsoever, while black-eyed specimens are not true albinos. This can get a little confusing, as what looks like a black-eyed white mouse may, in fact, be what is classed as a Cream, an "off-white" mouse with black eyes.

Other popular Self varieties include Black, Chocolate, Dove (a soft gray color), Red Fawn (a pale orangey color), Champagne (the color of "champagne silk," as in the Mouse Standards), and Blue (a medium slate-blue color).

TANS

The Tan group consists of mice with a recognized top color and a tan belly, defined as being of a "rich golden hue" in the Standards. In good show specimens, the top color and the tan color must be clearly separated by a straight demarcation line. Tans are extremely attractive mice, often to be found for sale.

MARKED

There are quite a few

varieties covered by this group, although some, such as the Even-Marked and Rump White, are rare. Breeding Marked Mice to a correct standard, in which the markings must conform as closely as possible, is, as you can imagine, quite a difficult task. There are very few mice in a litter that do conform to the standard.

The most commonly found Marked varieties are:

Broken Marked—a white mouse with seven or eight large spots of color on its body.

Dutch—a very attractive specimen with a patch covering each side of the face, separated by a white blaze. The neck and shoulders are white, joined by a colored saddle extending to the rump and down half of the tail and back legs. This is an exacting standard, with lots of mismarked results, which can also be very appealing to the pet mouse owner.

Variegated—another white mouse, with patches of color splashed evenly over its body.

Banded—a colored mouse with a white band around its midriff.

ANY OTHER COLOR

There are a great many different varieties listed under this grouping. Some are quite exotic; many are quite rare. Again, there are a few of these varieties that are most likely to be found in pet shops:

Seal Point Siamese—rather like the original Siamese cat, the body being colored medium beige, shading gradually down to a dark point at the tail root. Darker seal points are also to be found on the muzzle, ears, and feet.

Agouti—often said to resemble the wild mouse but in reality a lot more attractive than that, with rich brown to golden fur, ticked with black.

Cinnamon—a related color of Agouti but more of a rust-golden tan and brown, instead of black, ticking.

Chinchilla—naturally enough, this variety is named after the chinchilla itself—or rather the original form of this animal. It is colored mid gray, with a slate-blue undercoat and an intermediate shade of pearl gray, with each hair evenly tipped with black.

COAT VARIETIES

The different coat variations in mice are extremely interesting and attractive. These mice may be any standard recognized color variety but have different fur types, by which they are primarily judged. They are as follows:

Satin—a relatively recently developed variety, with the standard being granted to Mr. and Mrs. A. and G. Cooke in 1975. Satins have a coat with a high sheen, resulting in "an exquisite satin-like or metallic gloss," as stated in the N.M.C. Standard. They really are quite sensational and make highly attractive pets as well as exhibition animals.

Astrex—This is the oldest known "coat variety," developed by Mr. A. Tuck. The standard was granted to him back in 1936. The mouse's coat is extremely curly, often wavy, with the whiskers also curled. Unfortunately, although youngsters often have wonderfully tightly curled fur, this often straightens out with various molts by the time they are adult. It is still possible to discern that they are Astrex, but they are often a pale imitation of younger animals. Occasionally, a particular specimen, usually a buck, will retain good curling into adulthood. Needless to say, specimens like this are the ones to breed.

Longhaired—This is the second oldest variety in this category, with the standard being granted to Mr. A. D. Jones in 1969. As the name suggests, this variety has long fur, as long and as dense as possible, being of silky texture. As in hamsters, Longhaired bucks have noticeably longer coats than do does.

Rex—This curly-coated variety is not to be confused with the Astrex. Its curls are much closer and denser, almost fuzzy.

Young Rex mice have a rather disconcerting appearance, looking almost bald for a number of weeks before their fur molts into its final adult form. Even then, the animal's skin can be clearly seen through the close curls of the coat!

Despite this, however, the Rex is a fascinating, if neglected, variety and is currently enjoying a revival of interest among some fanciers. The provisional standard was originally granted to Mrs. E. Branston in 1975 but lapsed due to lack of fanciers' interest in developing the variety. Currently, the variety has been taken up and developed by Mr. Nick Baxter but remains unstandardized.

The different Coat Varieties make highly attractive pets, especially as they can also be bred in combination with one another, such as Satin Longhaired, Satin Astrex or even Longhaired with Satin Astrex.

RARE VARIETIES

As previously mentioned, several of the more specialist varieties of mouse are also quite rare. These mice really are the province of more experienced fanciers, but, of course, there is always a slim possibility that some may become available from a breeder as sub-show standard but perfectly acceptable pet-quality animals. So look out for varieties such as Dove, Pearl, Rump White, Tricolor, Blue Point Siamese, and the latest new mutation, the Brindle. The Brindle deserves a special mention, being a most unusual variety. It appears almost "marbled," the Standard calling for the mouse to "have streaks, bars, and little ears of any color over a diluted background." Unfortunately, this is one of those varieties with a rare "lethal" genetical factor: only Brindle does survive into adulthood and may be bred. Any bucks usually die within two weeks of birth. This obviously presents a problem insofar as correct breeding is concerned. Breeders use a standard colored buck to mate with a Brindle doe to create a mixture of Brindle and "normal"-colored offspring. The provisional standard was granted to Steve Haswell in 1990.

THE MOUSE FANCY'S BEGINNINGS

The first fancy mice were shown in England in 1892 at a show in Oxford. The fact that mouse classes were staged at this show was widely reported in the fanciers' newspaper *Fur & Feather*. This led to several interested mouse breeders getting together and exhibiting mice at a few more shows. By 1895, their numbers had swelled sufficiently to enable them to form a proper mouse club to cater to their needs. Thus it was in December 1895 that the British Mouse Club was founded. The club's name changed the following year to the National Mouse Club (N.M.C.), by which name it is known to this day. Nowadays, the N.M.C. acts as the governing body of the mouse fancy in the UK and has several regional mouse clubs

affiliated with it. These clubs stage regular shows in their own particular areas. Although not a terribly complex hobby, mouse fancying deserves more than a few lines in this book to describe it.

EXHIBITING MICE

If you decide that you want to take your interest in fancy mice further than merely keeping them as pets and breeding them, then your best approach is to join the mouse fancy and actually exhibit mice at shows.

The prospective mouse fancier should read about shows in more specialized publications and make direct contact with his local mouse club. This gives you a unique chance to meet other folks with the same interest as yourself. Shows provide a great social forum for people from all walks of life to meet, talk, and show mice. Experienced mouse fanciers will nearly always be ready and willing to impart advice and practical help from their knowledge of mice. However, do remember one thing: *If you ask for advice, be prepared to listen to more experienced fanciers and act on what you are told.* Above all, once you start showing mice and actively participating in the club's affairs, you will gain a great sense of enjoyment and fun, which is born out of good sportsmanship and friendly competition. Best of luck!

Health

As with any pet animal's health, prevention is always better than cure. Prevention in this case is proper care, or husbandry, to use the correct term. Always ensure that your mice are housed under clean conditions and that the housing is cleaned regularly; that they are fed the correct diet; and that they are kept at an even temperature. In short, use common sense. Of course, sometimes even with the most lavish care and attention, mice can fall ill. Often this is not the fault of their owner. Sometimes illnesses can be hereditary or caught from infected mice at shows. Your mice can even catch colds from you!

A complete list of possible ailments and their treatment would be impossible in a book this size. What follows is a brief list of the major ailments of mice, with notes about their possible treatment.

WOUNDS

Mice usually coexist quite happily in correctly structured groups. Occasionally, however, for whatever reason, fights can occur, more often than not between two bucks. They seldom lead to the death of either protagonist but can lead to wounds that will need to be treated. An untreated wound may get dirty and flare up into an abscess or even lead to a blood infection.

Remove the mouse from its cage and gently bathe its wounds in warm water. If the wound looks particularly dirty, a very small amount of diluted antiseptic may be added to the water with which you clean it. If the wound has developed into an abscess, it will need to be opened and emptied. This is done by gently squeezing any pus out into a tissue. Be careful not to squeeze too hard and hurt the mouse—it may go into shock. The abscess will then need to be bathed. To make completely sure that all pus is cleared out of the abscess, a drop of hydrogen peroxide will do the trick. Apply it to the abscess cavity, where it will bubble up upon contact with the flesh, forcing all the pus out of the cavity.

MITES

These small fur-dwelling parasites can occasionally be brought in with untreated hay or sawdust, as well as by infected mice. Treatment is twofold. First, you will need to dip your mouse in a parasiticide, which may be obtained from a pet shop or a veterinarian. One dip should be enough to eliminate most of the mites on the mouse.

Next, a special "fly block," or pest strip, which will kill any remaining mites in the area, will need to be placed in the same room as the mouse's cage. Again, prevention is better than cure, so always have such a device set up if possible.

DIARRHEA

The symptoms of diarrhea are very obvious—and smelly. This points to too much greenfood or liquid food being given to your mouse. Simply cut out all vegetables, fruit, and "wet" food for a few days and feed only plain dry mix, with fresh drinking water always available. The condition should soon right itself. After a week or so, you can start feeding the greens again but in smaller quantities than before. If the condition persists, it may be due to a bacterial infection, in which case consult your vet.

COLDS

The symptoms of a cold in mice are the same as in humans: runny nose, sneezing, hunched-up appearance, lethargy, and sore eyes. Isolate a mouse with a cold in its own cage in a warmer environment, with extra bedding. Feed it some nutritious supplement, such as bread and milk with cod-liver oil and extra vitamins added. The cold should soon disappear, and, after a week or so, the mouse can be returned to a communal cage.

CONCLUSION

Properly cared for, a mouse can make a very interesting pet. It will compensate for its short life span by packing a lot of activity into its life, and thus it will give you a great deal of amusement and enjoyment. If you decide to breed mice, then, from your original pair or trio, you can create your own mouse dynasty and chart the development of colors and markings throughout each generation. If you move into showing mice, then a whole world of interest and enjoyment in the mouse fancy awaits you. It is all up to you, so enjoy the delights and pleasures of...Your First Mouse.

SUGGESTED READING

T.F.H. Publications offers the most comprehensive selection of books dealing with mice. A selection of significant titles is presented below; they and many other works are available from your local pet shop.

Fancy Mice
by Chris Henwood
KW-224
ISBN 0-86622-342-8

Mice as a Hobby
by Jack Young
TT-019
ISBN 0-86622-949-3

Mice as a New Pet
by Richard Pfarr
TU-022
ISBN 0-86622-530